HOLLY

HOLLY

grace (ge) gilbert

YESYES BOOKS · PORTLAND

INTERIOR ART: GRACE (GE) GILBERT
COVER DESIGN: KATIE PRINCE
INTERIOR DESIGN: GRACE (GE) GILBERT AND KATIE PRINCE
PROJECT LEAD: KMA SULLIVAN AND GALE MARIE THOMPSON
AUTHOR PHOTO: LUIZA FOLEGATTI

ISBN: 978-1-946303-17-2
PRINTED IN THE UNITED STATES OF AMERICA

PUBLISHED BY YESYES BOOKS
PORTLAND, OR
YESYESBOOKS.COM

Table of Contents

On October 6, 1976, in Watertown, New York, a thirty-four-year-old woman was strangled with her own pantyhose and shot in the neck and head in her own kitchen.

Her nine- and eleven-year-old sons found her body upon returning home from a Scout meeting.

The eleven-year-old boy is my father.

for Holly, whom I carry

II.

YOU left me, sweet, two legacies,—
A legacy of love
A Heavenly Father would content,
Had He the offer of;

You left me boundaries of pain
Capacious as the sea,
Between eternity and time,
Your consciousness and me.

HOLLY AS COMING INTO MY CONSCIOUSNESS RATHER ABRUPTLY

Through a brittle, yellowed Ziploc full of hair.

It was dislodged somehow from a scrapbook, perched on a kitchen shelf that seemed to be miles above my head, and fell awkwardly to the linoleum in front of me.

The terse, uneven curl of my father's first attempt at a haircut grazes my chin. I am wearing an ill-fitting sweatshirt with ambiguously stained sleeves, which boasts the words BOWLING GREEN STATE UNIVERSITY—my mother's alma mater. I wear this almost every day, in the way children do—picking something with no certain significance to latch onto as if it were something essential.

I stand, a child and a bag of hair, before my curiosity brings me into a squat on the checkered linoleum, the baggie resting between my mismatched socks.

The hair, even through the dull film of aged plastic, is noticeably lush and curly. It gives off a sort of honeyed sheen, not too far off from the color of my own hair, though mine is frustratingly thin, wiry, and prone to chaos ("Did you even BRUSH your hair?" my mother yells almost daily as we are on our way out the door). ▾

I don't have much of a moment to consider a reaction—my mother enters the kitchen, and, somehow with a two-year-old and a laundry basket in tow, swiftly collects the baggie from between my feet.

"Don't play with that. It's your grandmother's," she snaps, and I place it in my still-developing toy box of facts that, perhaps, every six-year-old in our neighborhood has encountered a small baggie full of their dead grandmother's hair.

Republican leader's wife slain
NOV

HOLLY AS EVERY MORNING AND EVERY EVENING, THE SCENE IS THE SAME

My father takes part in a ritual at the mantle.

Here a black-and-white portrait of my grandmother rests, the only frame among the handful of family photos—my sister in a pumpkin patch, my mother holding my infant-self inches from the shore of Lake Erie, a still of my siblings and me baby-limbed and shirtless, running through a sprinkler—that remains dust-free, wholly centered, wholly kept.

Tucked behind the silvered frame is an orange pop-cap prescription bottle, the label so faded its original intent is illegible. My father unscrews the cap and dips a finger inside, where a small well of holy water brims below the label's edge.

With a slight genuflect he smudges a tiny cross (up, down, left, right) on the image of my grandmother's forehead.

He mumbles some words. I never quite make out what he says. When he turns away from the brick façade, I make myself small as can be in the stairwell.

There is a mutual secrecy, a quiet logic to our ritual.

I never quite know what he says.

He never quite knows I am watching.

were saying words such as "tragic" and "awful" after learning of the murder, but the words didn't begin to capture the shock and fear they were experiencing.

The quiet, affluent neighborhood was crowded with parked cars and small groups of persons standing on sidewalks, doorsteps and peering ... behind windows ...

As word-of-mouth spread news of the murder, husbands began driving home in mid-afternoon to be with their families and to learn what had happened.

One woman, out from the neighborhood, told her husband: "We're going to get that garage door lock fixed."

Downtown workers and customers this morning were still ...

"I've never heard it so quiet here," she said. "There wasn't a sound for 15 minutes."

Not only was the murder in the neighborhood so shocking to the residents, but it also was equally surprising that none of them had apparently heard or seen anything suspicious.

entire road and the front lawns are clearly visible.

North of the home is a turn-around for cars with ...

Agway Petroleum
will be closed
Mon., Oct. 11
In Observance Of
Columbus Day

REVERA
FRI. SPECIAL
Canadian
Bullhead Dinner
$3.50 W/Full Salad Bar

PUFF'S
ICE CREAM
It's Time Again for
Egg Nog
Soft Ice Cream

Rodman
Cheese Factory
Will Not Have
Cheese For Sale
Until Nov. 1, 1976

Watertown
...er Skating
Rink

Dine & Dance
OLYMPIA REST.
Friday Special
FRIED FILLET of HADDOCK $2.50
W/French Fries & Salad

TONIGHT
"Steak N...

HOLLY AS SOMEDAY DADDY WILL TELL YOU

I ask my mother what "virgin" means
I ask my mother if the F word is "fox"
I ask my mother why we live next to an onion farm

I ask my mother why I have my name
I ask my mother why she has her name
I ask my mother why it smells like onions when it rains

I ask my mother why bologna looks like that
I ask my mother why people have to say 'please'
I ask my mother for a vanilla wafer

I ask my mother why I am not a boy
I ask my mother how many miles the sky is
I ask my mother why she drives with one hand

I ask my mother why babies are bald
I ask my mother if it's safe to eat pennies
I ask my mother why she has a pottymouth

I ask my mother why the road looks like that when it's hot
I ask my mother about Gramma
I ask my mother if Gramma died in a car accident

I ask my mother if Gramma died from being too cold
I ask my mother if Gramma died from being too warm
I ask my mother if Gramma gets bored sometime [illegible]

I ask my mother if Gramma

There are never words
for the quiet
There was never a sound
he body of Holly C. Gilbert is taken
the Gilbert e at 1214 Ha

HOLLY AS RECOVERED SUNKEN MEMORY AS TORN HOLE IN THE MOTHER INSTINCT

When I start family therapy as a young teenager and am asked to try to recollect my early family unit, I realize I have no memory of my parents interacting with one another. None at all.

Just separate memories of Father or Mother, small image-bursts among the deep silence.

I have Mother memories, full of talk and warmth and image. Father memories are spare. Never conversations, just proximity, texture, observation—drives to school with my father, Frank Sinatra and Elton John sputtering through the CD-player in his Nissan Altima.

I remember the car seat, singing "Bennie and the Jets" with him in two-part harmony.

I remember sitting on the porch in the springtime, barefoot, as my father shot golf balls across the lawn.

I remember the hours, the fireflies, the light they made, as I ran to retrieve every ball for him.

I remember his smell—spiced cologne and coins.

I remember sitting in the church pews, the way he genuflected with a seriousness before the big wooden crucifix. The way I tried to imitate.

I remember his anger when I interrupted him, asked him one too many questions, his insistence that he heard me the first time.

I remember his hands when he gave me a bath, pouring gallons of water over my head in cool, aggravated succession. The water gurgling between my lips. Longing instead for the hands of my mother.

I remember the push, the shove, the lock of the bathroom door, the pounding, the silent steps down the hallway, the rush of my mother's arms.

I remember being pulled aside in class for writing about my favorite memory, fishing with my father on Lake Ontario, which never happened. The teacher asking me why I lied.

I remember losing a locket with my father's face in it between the leather seats of his car.

I remember crying, crying.

Crying for that loss.

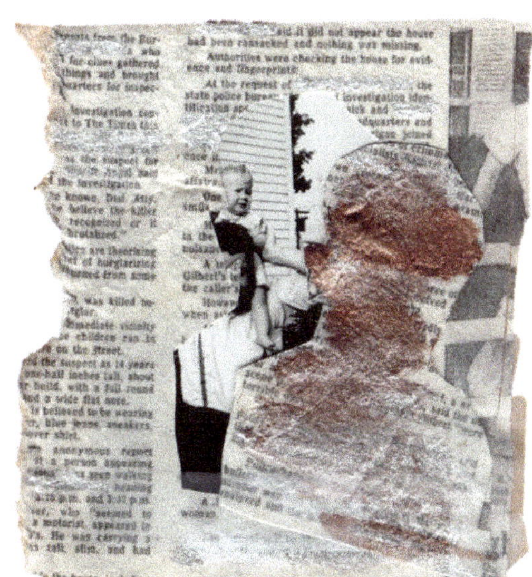

HOLLY AS MOTHER AND FATHER FALLING IN LOVE AT A GROCERY STORE

Summer, 1990.

Father is fresh out of law school, saddled with debt. He makes a living chopping vegetables at a supermarket in Watertown, New York.

He is twenty-five and thickset, with bad eyesight and a bulk of brown curls. He wears a smudged apron and wields a serrated knife, hacking away at an enamel cutting board behind the deli counter.

I imagine Mother in a pastel linen jumpsuit with thin, teased auburn hair that pops out of her head with a rigid persistence. She holds a yellow clutch, her big brown eyes painted with kohl-black eyeliner.

It's a setup, the initial meeting.

Mother, also twenty-five, spent her entire life in mid-Ohio—the part that's so flat it's maddening—and while visiting her cousin, Susan, was convinced to tag along for a grocery trip. Susan spent three years dating Father's younger brother, and, in a desperate attempt to win him back, decided to rope Mother into her scheme.

Mother finds herself at the deli counter with Susan throwing around a few phrases of feigned surprise—what a coincidence, the lot of them in the same tired building.

Mother purchases some sliced deli turkey and a cucumber. Father makes a joke about nearly chopping his finger off. Mother makes a joke about dropping the turkey on the ground, so she would have to hang around the counter just a bit longer.

There's some flirting, some self-conscious banter—a woman adjusting the straps on her jumpsuit, a man wiping his hands on his apron, leaving a trail of rinds.

Since childhood I've had a hard time differentiating between lying and unfulfilled desire.

And without any other options, even long after the love had gone, these are the truths I've kept.

the word
"mineral" and a sky
so vast my heart aches

HOLLY AS GENEALOGY OF LOSS

Holly's mother's name was Ann.

Ann, my great-grandmother, powdered lighthouse of sorrow.

Ann whose only son, grief-stricken, converted to Mormonism and ran far away from home.

Ann who raised my father when his father couldn't recover from Holly's death:

Ann who outlived her only daughter by over thirty years.

Ann who dies when I am seven years old. Ann who has dementia, which runs in the family. Ninety-three. It's so bad she forgets to breathe.

For a while Ann called my father and wished him a happy birthday.

In the beginning he said: "No Grandma, my birthday is in April."

Toward the end: "Thank you Grandma. Thank you."

At Ann's wake we sit in a small room in a big church.

Everything is burgundy, even the faces, the leather crawling across the Bibles and hymnals and the missal my father keeps unprovoked in his lap.

My sister and I ask every attendee for their business card. We trade them secretly in the hallway.

We keep away from the mourning, from the silvered ringlets of the dead woman's hair.

At one point Holly's widow, my grandfather, stands to give a speech. The room a dry, stifled cough.

He bows before the casket.

"Thank you for giving me your daughter, so I could have my sons."

Ann remains curled, powdered, still. I look up at my father, his hand on the leather-bound missal, his eyes glazed straight ahead.

Ann who could never tell me what happened to Holly—by the time I was old enough to speak, she was too old to remember how.

Ann who died having forgotten that she ever had a daughter at all.

wife slain

a loss
at close range
violent
neighborhood
Her body
beginning
and ending
where the body was found
(far right) talks to
Richard S.
Drive following the murder of his wife,
Holly, Wednesday afternoon. Friends and
neighbors wait at the left to console Gil-
bert, who is also the Jefferson County
publican Committee chairman

HOLLY AS LEARNING METAPHOR

Anne Carson said it well— "kinds of water drown us, kinds of water do not."

It's September when the flood comes that washes away my parents' marriage.

At least that's what it feels like.

As an eight-year-old I take to journaling, to poetry. There's not much choice in it. Everywhere, I see images that act as organizing facts in my life.

One weekend, my father packs up his baseball hats, trading cards, scrapbooks, the photo of Holly on the mantle.

That same weekend, it must have rained for forty hours straight.

When our basement gives in to the demands of the rain, my sisters and I put on waders.

We watch as a slow, crude slideshow of our childhood drifts by—our dolls, toys, our photographs set to some sluggish, unforgettable motion.

I write often of floods.

The flood that seeps in around the edges of my childhood, the Biblical flood my father warns us of, the deep-river flood that carries away my friend's body while I am in college.

And what is it that's so devastating about water?

Perhaps it's a fear that nothing about water is new—everything so old,
collected, mildewed and floating at a water-dull pace.

It's all there, the history, the sediment—photographs of my parents when they
felt more in love and less devastated by it, where my mother was thin with kohl-
black eyeliner and my father was the wall she stood against.

Where nothing felt curt and final as the papers they held to each other, the
manila folders I found hidden deep beneath piles of my mother's knit sweaters,
things she kept ready for winter.

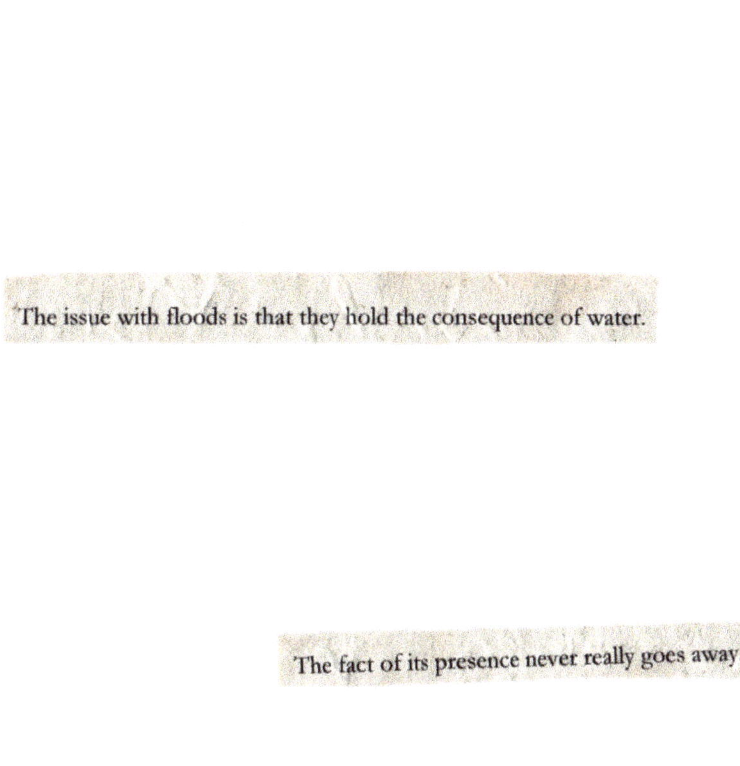

The issue with floods is that they hold the consequence of water.

The fact of its presence never really goes away.

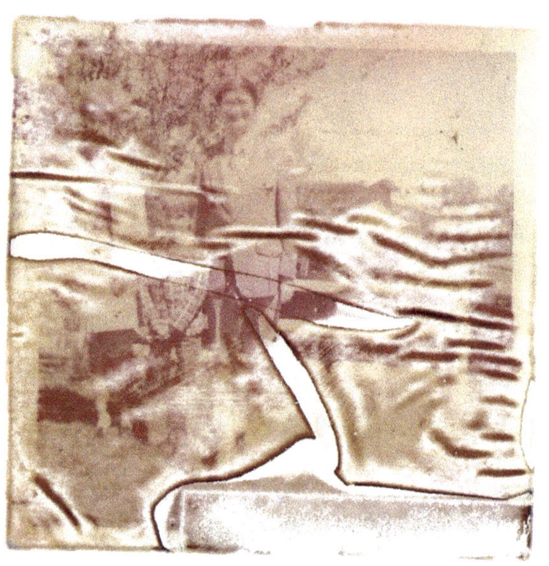

After the flood, the pulp of basement is a raw exhibit of our new life.

It becomes the very architecture of our family—the exposed beams soft and suppled through with memories of water; walls cut below the waterline, boxes here and there to gather the things we must keep but have nowhere to put on display.

Photos, books, albums—all yellowed with age, plagued by water that came somewhere from the ground and into our home, water that broke our pipes and pumps and machines and buckets—water that washed through and left the echo of a family, rotting.

I was afraid of my father's preoccupation with holy water—its scent like old pennies and leftover incense, the many gods and hands and ghosts it must've passed through to get to my father and then to me.

Often, on the way home from mass, from the backseat, I could look into the rearview mirror and see the tips of my father's ears, his strong eyebrows, the sternness of a forehead that held the watermark of a God he loved.

Bits of rain and oil.

The beginnings of hair that curled into itself, faded deeply into a graying black.

Sometimes, his eyes would glance into the rearview and, for a moment, we would meet, collected in our own intimate space, before I remembered that there were many, many things behind me that took up the entire depth of his gaze.

And when I turned around to see them, all I could see was rain coming down.

I had a father who loved the water of a God who sent

the flood. I had a father in the seat of history.

I had a father with hands that seemed

Biblical. I had a father that scared me.

I had a father that made me wonder—is every father a kind

of water? And what if that water was a flood?

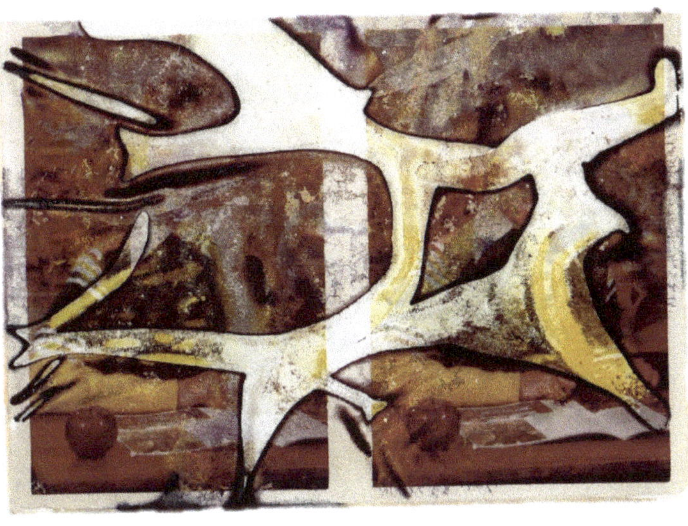

There are many floods in literature, so much that rides in on the flow of the symbol, and yet when I stand knee-deep in the flood of my family home, I feel some new form of disaster.

Every flood is new.

It fills a space and eats its language.

It carries objects like a museum; everything brought to the surface in a strange moment of preservation, a series of facts set to the pace of water.

Curled at the fifth stair, toes above the waterline, I watch my world of objects linger around me like symbols.

And they stay like that, my thoughts.

Deep in some places, filled with the sluggish vestiges of a father, of a home, of a past I know nothing of and yet feel so deeply I think myself to be drowning.

XXII.

THE bustle in a house
    The morning after death
Is solemnest of industries
Enacted upon earth,–

The sweeping up the heart,
And putting love away
We shall not want to use again
Until eternity.

HOLLY AS CUSTODY AGREEMENT

My father takes us to a mattress store. He picks out three beds and three bed frames.

On the way to his new place, we go through the Burger King drive-thru for three cheeseburgers and three small cartons of fries.

The apartment is temporary, he says, until he can find a nice big house to rent, one where we can each have our own bedroom.

It's evidently college housing—at certain times of night, the window looks out over hordes of young adults either walking eagerly toward the bars or staggering back home, shoes in hand.

My room doesn't have a door.

At night, I keep thinking I hear rats clawing through the wall next to my head.

I imagine a dozen of them plowing a hole through the crumbling plaster while I sleep. I imagine them leaping onto my small body, bearing it through with holes.

When I wake from the nightmare, I drag my blanket and pillow across the hall and lay them on the floor between my sisters' twin bedposts, where I sleep every night we have visitation for almost a year.

One Saturday afternoon, my sisters & I pile onto the pullout couch as my father bends over to finagle with the VHS player, bits of dust peeking out between his graying curls.

My father wants to show us home videos from when he was a child, videos he packed up before he left.

The videos are compiled in choppy, flickering bursts, all from the early to mid 70s.

My father and his brother standing and waving from the top of a ten-foot snow pile, the boys in matching overalls pulling one another in a red wagon, the boys running in circles in the driveway before their first day of school.

The last shot I remember shows my grandmother, thirty-four, in a sleek two-piece swimsuit and a visor that hardly contains a mess of blonde curls.

She stands, thigh-deep, in water, perhaps a small lake; as she notices the camera, she poses playfully with her arms thrown wide—her smile evident against the blue.

The time stamp reads July, 1976.

"This was from your grandma and grandpa's anniversary," my father notes from his seat on the chipped hardwood floor, his lips upturned in a sort of sad smile, one I'd seen hundreds of times before, but never quite like this.

61

(252)

I can wade Grief –
Whole Pools of it –
I'm used to that –
But the least push of Joy
Breaks up my feet –

HOLLY AS MOURNING AND MELANCHOLY

I was born, snug and boyish, between two sisters.

We fell at ease into a staggered, podium-like formation.

The youngest was the closest to an angel on earth—she had bright blonde curls and moved about her life with the burden of youth and attention. The oldest was brilliant but painfully shy. She played violin, read a lot of books. She did everything first and perfectly while remaining, emotionally, like absolute stone.

In the middle, I was so high off the ground it beguiled me. I was emotionally labile, needy, nervous, what my mother called "the nut".

Whether she meant crazy, or queer, or a shell that held something small and critical, I have yet to figure out.

Despite our uneven standing, girlhood was our marker, what kept us aligned and in view of one another, what defined our family as we walked through churches, grocery stores, rest stops, three ducks in a line behind our forward-marching mother.

It was a standard that kept us together, our weft.

And yet even that I couldn't quite fit into.

I remember at a childhood friend's birthday party, between games that involved glitter eyeshadow and conceptual dessert that involved gummy worms, I sat around the kitchen table with a host of other children.

"Are you a *TOM*-boy?" The girl next to me asked, chin tilted, drawling out the word like it was a piece of chewing gum she couldn't quite make into a bubble.

"My mommy said that girls that dress like you are called *TOM*-boys."

My identity was as confusing as the benefits it seemed to provide.

For one, being a boy kept me, rather obviously, in closer ranks with my father than my sisters.

My memories of tenderness and togetherness with my father revolve around learning the proper ways to perform.

He would wake me up early, just me, and bring me to driving ranges, empty fields, oval tracks.

He would hand me heavy wooden baseball bats, set up distant soccer goals and labyrinthine sequences of orange cones.

He would spend hours in windbreakers teaching me how to putt, shoot, throw, run, practice, react, until I had done something that proved something I wasn't quite sure I was trying to prove.

"Gracer throws just like a boy," he would say proudly at family gatherings, pulling me in for a one-armed hug, my knees dirty and bony and hairy like they knew exactly the conditions of the role.

replays of the
present
selves
Apart

Like Judith Butler, I believe that our rigidity around gender spawns a particular form of melancholy.

It's a mourning for something that never really died but never really lived either, mourning with a lack of direction or language.

All I knew was that, as I got older, I became less of a tomboy and more a signifier of something uncomfortable for others.

I was bullied in school, mostly by one girl from whom I learned the term *lezzy*, a seemingly secret and terrible insult among the fourth grade.

I learned to stabilize through self-loathing, through mimicry, my rivers.

I grew out and straightened my hair, tossed my father's caps and the cutoffs my mother made for me, lied to my friends about a period that I didn't get until I was fifteen, matured into the other form, took place.

It was a deep something I felt when I saw what I'd become. For the rest of my performance as a girl I could hardly look.

A soft field with no footholds, nowhere to land.

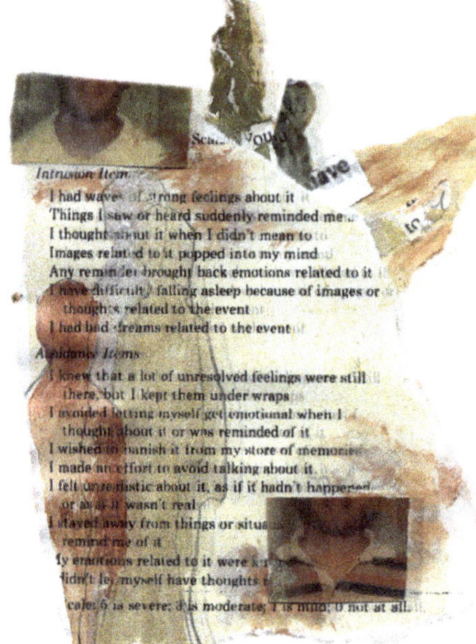
you
have
I had waves
feelings about it
Things I saw or heard suddenly reminded me
I thought
it when I didn't mean to
Images
to it popped into my mind
Any
back emotions related to it
falling asleep because of images or
related to the event
related to the event
I knew that a lot of unresolved feelings were still
there, but I kept them under wraps
thought
about it or was reminded of it
from my store of
I made
to avoid talking about it.
about it, as if it hadn't
wasn't real
away from things or
remind me of it
related to it were
myself have thoughts
is severe;
moderate;
not at all.

Susan died when I was eighteen. Before that, she taught me how to drive in the dark.

In high school, I'd spend weekends up in Watertown with her as an alternative form of custody. I had my mother, but Susan was my web—my warm connection to the tenuous pasts of both my parents. It was an invaluable relationship–she had a surrogate child, I had access to answers I didn't feel I could get anywhere else.

I drove her Subaru up and down the bleak Northern highway, the air so bitter and black I made a habit of staring at the white lines on the side of the road just to have something to fill the shock of darkness.

At sixteen, knuckles white and taut against the wheel, I sat next to my aunt who told me how she had run into my father at the courthouse recently, how he had gushed about my performance at a track meet.

"I think he's always wanted to attach a penis to you," she said, half-absentmindedly.

"It's like he wants to relive some semblance of his boyhood."

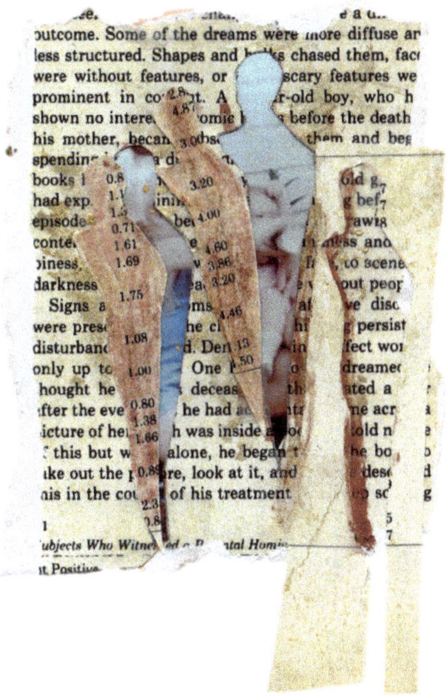

outcome. Some of the dreams were more diffuse ar
less structured. Shapes and b…s chased them, face
were without features, or … scary features we
prominent in co…t. A …r-old boy, who h
shown no intere… …omic … before the death
his mother, becan… …obs… them and beg
spendin… … a d…
books … 0.8 … 3.20 …old g
had exp… 1.1 … …inin… g bef
episode … 1.3 … be… 4.00 … rawi
conte… 0.71 … e … 4.60 … ness and
piness, 1.61 … 3.86 … to scene
darkness 1.69 … pa… 3.20 … out peop
Signs a… 1.75 … oms … 4.46 … ve disc
were pres… … he cl… …hi… g persist
disturbanc… 1.08 … d. Den… 13 … in… ffect wor
only up to… 1.00 … One … 4.50 … dreamed
hought he … deceas… …th… …ated a
fter the eve… 0.80 … he had a… …me acr
icture of he… 1.38 … h was inside a … told n
this but w… 1.66 … alone, he began t… …he bo
ake out the p… 0.8… re, look at it, and … des
is in the cou… of his treatment … sc
1 … 2.3 … 5
… 0.8 … 7

ubjects Who Witne…ed a P…ntal Homi…

t Positive

Freud suggests that in mourning, we mourn the loss of a loved object. In melancholia, we mourn the loss of an idea.

This loss, this mourning is what first connected me to poetry, to lyricism, to the melancholics of past and present.

This is also how I connect to my father.

My melancholy created a field for me—joy an interesting divot, a deep hole in a colorless sea of flowers.

I felt the adults in my life could sense this.

I listened as a woman from church told me about her pain from her divorce, I listened as my family therapist described the abyss of loneliness she felt as she aged, and I listened when my mother took me on errands and confided in me about my father's wrongdoings, the anger she felt from his absence.

I remember thumbing my way through a Sally Beauty Supply, the scent of plastic hair extensions and nail polish remover creating an aura of brassy femininity. I still felt nauseous in the car, a new matte black nail polish in tow, as my mom described the emotional emptiness of my father.

"It's like there's a cog missing," she said.

"Something's just not quite there."

I long for

[illegible] don't ask [illegible] did [illegible] down

[illegible]

I don't ask about that memory [illegible]

think I inherited th[illegible]

[illegible] blonde hair. Her [illegible] a [illegible]

[illegible]d scratch that lasts forever

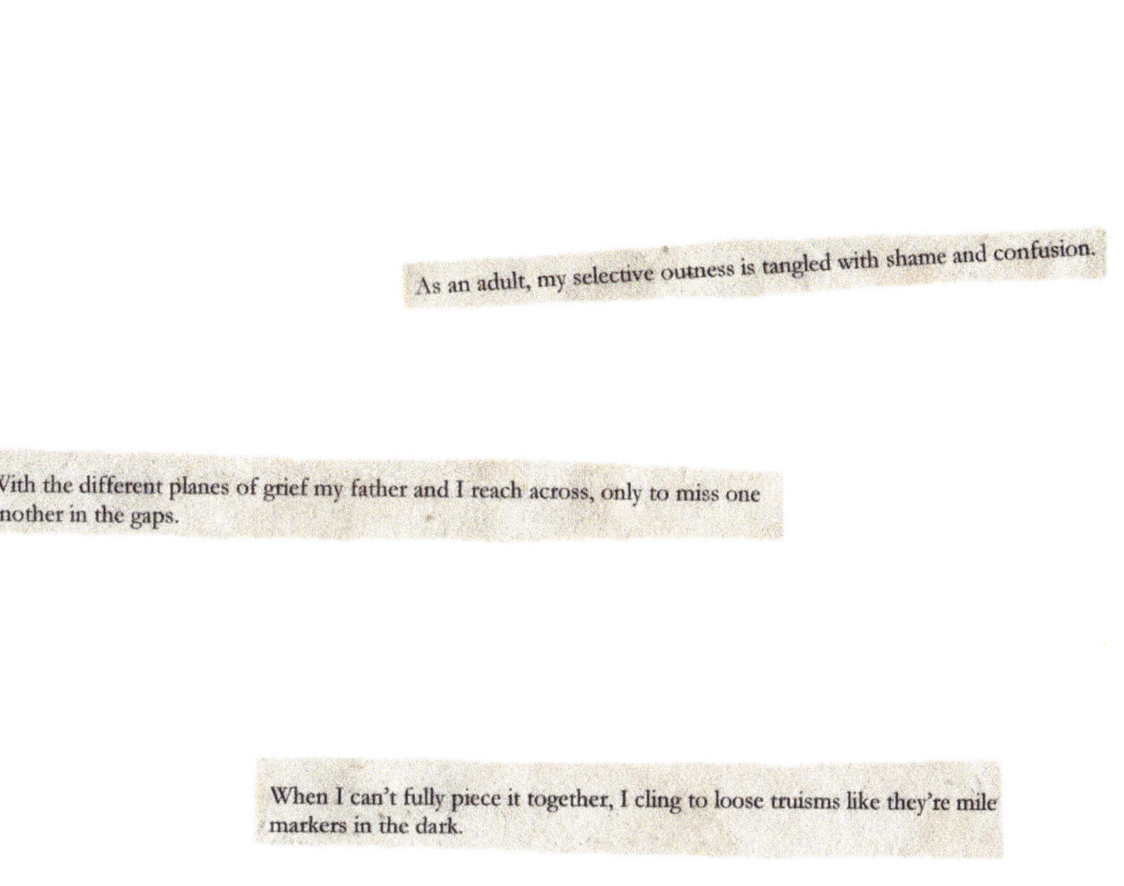
As an adult, my selective outness is tangled with shame and confusion.
With the different planes of grief my father and I reach across, only to miss one another in the gaps.
When I can't fully piece it together, I cling to loose truisms like they're mile markers in the dark.

What I know: that certainty itself is a kind of sadness.

That ontological incoherence is itself a form of grief.

XXXIII.
I MEASURE every grief I meet
I try to put her back.
The grieved are
is but one
And only nail

HOLLY AS BOYS RUNNING IN TWO DIRECTIONS

The plants I keep grow with a suddenness around me.

In their living stillness, I often feel the God my father kneels before in church—when nurtured, filling space.

In Karen Green's *Bough Down*, her two dogs run into the garage where she finds her husband hanging.

One dog comes up to sniff his owner's feet, whine and whimper at his limp shadow. The other runs away.

Reality itself feels like a myth that evaporates and leaves behind only pieces.

Living in her world of glass, hair, blood, cloth

Sometimes I wonder why she didn't fight harder.

Why she couldn't hold the knife with the power of mothers in literature, mothers in films, mothers who can move boulders with a single pinky full of love.

Sometimes these thoughts shoulder into her story until I remember that she was not just a mother, she was a self.

A self that had a moment where she knew she was going to die, and feeling the cold tile beneath her, let her self spill out as a self, all the roles of her floating out of her body and into the walls around her.

Into the bodies of her husband and her sons, into the lines that stretched from them.

"She was the glue," my father once told me in a rare moment of reflection.

"And when that glue dissolved, we had no idea how to stay together."

I am my father's grief born into a body

When he acted like it, I didn't flinch or hide

I knew somewhere inside this was my inheritance—he would either hold its bleeding head or run away.

And either way, this grief would burn and bloom in me like something formed below the earth. And with the urgency characteristic of living things, someday it would root up and break soil.

The two boys ran into the house and found their mother on the kitchen floor, bleeding from the head.
First
to
Know
The two boys ran
house and found
mother on the kitchen
bleeding from the head.
their
mother
bleeding
The boys ran

As a young teenager, I return what I see as neglect with icy silence. To his silence, I offer a fork scraped against a plate, a low-brimmed baseball cap covering my eyes, my crossed arms in the back of the van he shares with my new stepmother.

I craft scenarios where he is given the option to choose me—nasty fights with my stepsiblings, custody weekends I make sure to spend entirely at friends' houses, toeing the water with bad behavior that I am sure must provoke some sort of reaction.

But he never does choose me.

Instead, we drive together, silently, twenty minutes across town where he returns me to my mother.

In the backseat I wilt next to a pile of my stepbrother's basketball clothes, my stepsister's dance bag.

And later, when the callousness falls away and leaves that mangled pulp of self, I stare into my childhood bedroom mirror until I feel like I might evaporate.

Feature by feature, strand by strand.

My uncle is my father's inverse—blonde wispy hair, eyes like rain, like dishwater. Eyes like hers.

He married once, right after college, to a woman who loves him so much she absorbs his contented silence with laughter and antipasto.

Their house is large and full of trophies—dance, baseball, and the less evident, though louder, successes—a table set for four, gallery walls anchored by family photos, patient nods from the man at the table, patient hands.

I do not speak with my uncle much, but I intuit the foil. Visiting him feels parallel, as if I am walking in a world with familiar bones, but an unfamiliar body

I feel thick love, and an absence, when my uncle kisses his daughter goodnight.

I feel thick love, and an absence, when on Thanksgiving my aunt and uncle fell asleep together on the couch.

I feel thick love, and an absence, when I see my father's eyes and wish they were a different color.

This was my childhood: I felt thick love—and an absence.

This was his childhood: one dog stayed. One dog ran away.

no one hear-
ing the noises
boy

HOLLY AS FRAGMENT AS ROOM I COULD NEVER LEAVE

In their private, composed nature, neither of my parents could bear to give us the details.

Not about my grandmother, not about their separation, not about how any one thing had to do with something else.

It was too much.

For most of my childhood I made a habit of looking for answers on my own.

I peered through scrapbooks, filed through my mom's journals, and flipped my father's yellow legal pads. I scoured birthday cards and eavesdropped on phone calls through my father's thin, splintered bedroom door.

What I collected were fragments.

A bag of her hair, a framed photo, a ten-second video clip. My older sister's nose, my younger sister's cheekbones. My stature.

My father's sad, deep stare.

I could see her then.

A bright eclipse between us.

hush
hush
hush
hush hush
hush hush
hush hush hush
hush hush hush

HOLLY AS SIN OF OMISSION

It's Susan who finally tells me how it happened.

I am seventeen.

My mother's closest confidant, and mine, too, Susan sits me down prior to my first foray into University.

Our conversation takes place in Susan's gray Subaru, on the way to the Eastview Mall in Rochester, New York, where she is taking me to a Vera Bradley outlet to purchase a cheerful flower-patterned pill case.

This is a gesture intended to make me feel a bit less embarrassed about my newly corrupted brain chemistry—the long doctor's appointments, the family therapist I try to keep secret from my friends, the loose Xanax I keep in my windbreaker during track practice.

Something in my head had begun to click, and click, and click—a windup toy with nowhere to go.

Nights on end I sit in my bedroom closet for hours, arms wrapped around my knees, and feel shame for carrying so much emotion, emotion I can never share with my mother, my father, the small world I occupied.

I don't know if longstanding grief works in the logic of causation.

I don't know what caused what.

What it feels like is an arena, a thruway with a bundle of dizzying offshoots, a tangle of nerves.

Everything colors everything else, gray on gray, as Susan turns to me as we stall at a stoplight.

"She's a part of you," she says.

"So it's important that you know this part of you."

only then would
a
home
receive
death.

HOLLY AS PATRON SAINT OF POOR JUSTICE DELIVERY

I am nineteen when a man breaks into my college apartment.

It's two in the morning on a Saturday, alumni weekend, our backdoor unlocked in the veneer of rural safety. The man is white, and large.

He smells of soured beer and onions.

He is so intoxicated that he hardly makes it five steps into our kitchen before he blankets the white linoleum in vomit.

It's a simple game of time—for us, for him.

Ten steps, fifteen seconds in one direction and he would have reached the sound, sleeping bodies of my two housemates in their bunkbeds.

Twenty steps, thirty seconds up the carpeted stairs and he would have reached me, wearing only bloodstained underwear, leaning against my unlockable bedroom door with a wobbly hand over my mouth, trying not to breathe.

Luckily, we are on the winning side of time—a thud shuddering throughout the shoddy architecture of our old house—his large, hairy body lying prone on the living room floor.

When the campus police arrive, our yellow house is lit through with red and blue lights.

They pat the man on the back to wake him.

They call the man "buddy."

They say the man was just drunk and mistaken, that he didn't mean any harm.

When the police take the man away, I kneel on the floor and clean up his vomit. I pour bleach over the kitchen tiles, some of it splashing up my bare legs, singing the hairs I'd long neglected to shave. When I'm done, I curl up on the couch, terrified of sleep, and call my father, whom I've made a habit of calling only on birthdays or holidays.

My father's voice is an angle of him I've come to fear.

"If I have to drive down there myself and walk into that police department I will do so," he snarls through the phone.

"You sure as hell are pressing charges. No man breaks into my daughter's house and gets away with a pat on the back."

When we hang up, I wonder for the first time about Holly in terms of her luck, her circumstance, her justice.

I wonder if my father's vocation offers him a way to have some control over events like these—events that are so often dictated by time, by luck, by who happens to be in a room when a man wants to make decisions about power.

HOLLY AS FASHIONABLE NEIGHBORHOOD

My father's family grew up in a nice neighborhood in a poor, cold city in Northern New York.

I don't know too much about my grandmother. People tell me that she was pretty, loved Elton John, was active in her community. That she played tennis and walked in local fashion shows.

From what I gather by reading the newspaper clippings I've saved to my desktop, my grandmother's murderer grew up in the same nice neighborhood in the same cold city. He lived just down the street. He was fifteen when he stole a revolver, broke in, and killed her.

I try not to think about motive.

As it goes, he got eighteen months in juvey.

The word "inheritance" is rooted in the word "heir."

It means, in the most literal sense, to make an heir of someone.

The word "heir," though, traces back to the proto-Indo-European root *ghe*—it means "to be empty," or "to be left behind."

gunshots
Through

The grandmother in my head wears a turtleneck sweater, a brooch, foam curlers in her silvery-blonde hair.

I put some weight on her, some wrinkles, the corporeal signs of a life well worn.

She blushes often, laughs with a crudeness, and pats her adult sons on the back like they are still children. Her hands are raised and spread with a tenderness.

She welcomes this potential, this life that somehow flows into mine.

She says I love you, and she says thank you, *thank you*, and for a brief spell we are certain people in our certain place in our certain illusory time.

HOLLY AS LONG-DISTANCE PHONE CALL AS SEVENTEEN YEARS OF UNKNOWING AS INHERITED STONE SUNK DEEP

The form of my family—a sprawling map.

On my lunch break at the bakery, sitting beneath the walnut tree next to a lukewarm paper cup of black coffee.

I watch a couple chase their chubby, cheerful toddler through a garden.

I think of the weekend, the phone call with my mother.

My mother's voice a different state.

"You were just so young," she explains through the honeyed static between us.

"We didn't tell you because we didn't…we didn't know how to say it. What do you say to a child about murder?"

I wanted to respond saying that I understand, but instead it is a quiet, long anger I feel.

It is anger beneath the sun that feels viscous.

Anger within the summer that is grieving its own end.

Anger as the toddler reaches for the honeybee.

Anger as she is snatched immediately away, limbs pulsing in protest.

…ER—Pg. 11

In Court

11, of Harris Drive, appeared in Family Court Friday afternoon in relation to the Oct. 4 murder of Mrs. Holly A. Gilbert, 1214 Harris Drive.

District Attorney John Bastian said will be brought to trial the morning of Nov. 12 before Family Court Judge Angus Saunders.

However, because the juvenile's records have been sealed, Mr. Bastian said he could not comment on whether the youth [illegible] been charged in conn[illegible] with Mrs. Gilbert[illegible]

The [illegible] previously [illegible] charged [illegible] quenc[illegible] the t[illegible] hand[illegible] murd[illegible] stolen [illegible] the h[illegible]

[illegible]

caused smaller [illegible] pers to react erratically.

The powerfull pull of the crane magnet has strongly indicated to him that the missing gun is not there.

However, Mr. Bastian said he intended to go back to the spot this morning for a further search.

JOHN BASTIAN—He's getting the job done—Not just about it.—Adv.

the words — this is all i can do
this is all i can do

HOLLY AS SIXTH SENSE

Even though my shitty apartment is a rental, I'm trying to fix things up. I walk around with a measuring tape and a few ideas of how, finally, to make this place feel like a real home.

The divots in my office wall are peeling.

I put the plaster chips in a Ziploc bag.

This makes me think of my father.

The candlewick makes a beautiful, beautiful noise and I am thinking of my father.

It becomes apparent to me rather quickly that my imagination creates my expectations.

For example, I expect that I'll die young.

I feel I've inherited this.

At the dive bar, between puffs of a cigarette I can't stomach and a few hot toddies,
I tell my friend that I know life is short.

I know this because I've been given an inherited deadline.

In anticipation, I keep my door unlocked.

I make it easy for them.

Mrs. Gilbert was found fully clothed lying face down on the kitchen floor.

HOLLY AS SURVEY OF QUESTIONS FOR THE SURVIVED

In relation to you, who was the deceased?
Was the deceased fully clothed when found?
If so, what was she wearing?
Was the deceased fallen?
What angles did her body take?
Was the deceased found in the hallway, kitchen, bedroom, or foyer?
What was the deceased holding in her hand when she was murdered?
What song was the deceased humming before she was murdered?
What would the deceased think about the word *slain*?

What was the deceased planning for dinner that night?
Was the deceased wearing any jewelry when she was murdered?
How much did the deceased's pantyhose cost?
Was the deceased one to wear pantyhose past the first snag?
If not, where did she buy replacement pantyhose?
What happened to the deceased's pantyhose?
What is the deceased's full legal name?
Could the deceased whistle?
Could the deceased walk elegantly in high heels?
What book was on the deceased's nightstand?

Did the deceased have her hair done?
Did the deceased think of how her children needed haircuts?
Did the deceased think of her children?
Did the deceased think of anything?
Did the deceased run red lights if no one was watching?
Did the deceased prefer showers or baths?
What was the deceased's favorite restaurant?
Did the deceased like the sound of rain?
Did the deceased like poetry?
Did the deceased have dreams for herself?
Did the deceased have regrets?
What did the deceased do when no one was around?
Did the deceased like to dance?
Did the deceased read bedtime stories to her children?
Was the deceased read to as a girl?
What was the deceased's favorite subject in school?
Did the deceased have a crush?
Did the deceased like to party?
Was she drinking when?

Was she laughing when?
Was she crying
Did she cry out for her husband
Did she cry out for her sons
Did she cry out for her mommy
Did she cry out for you

C.
I hope we can stay in touch.

HOLLY AS OUR GRIEF OUR LONG ALGORITHMIC SPUTTER

My father has a golden retriever puppy.

A wife and two stepchildren.

I see him three times a year, at most.

My father gets grayer, balder, each time I see him. Rounder, a bit more sunken-in with life.

He is tactful and quiet. Adroit with a knife. Carving some meat, cutting some celery. He is half-smiling in the corner of a conversation. Brown eyes. Folding light away from the room.

Our cordial relationship plays out through social media. Passing screens. His face a pleasant and hopeful ghost.

Proud! his comment reads across a picture of his child sporting a cap and gown. *Beautiful!* on a photo of his child smiling broadly in the sun.

I log onto Facebook and am sent a reminder of my grandmother by an algorithm that consistently places me in the same digital house as my father.

His post appears first on my feed:

We lost our beautiful Mom 44 years ago today. The photo may be old and blurry, but it still provides many reasons to smile ♥. Be well everyone, and hug your Moms!

I forgot. Today is October sixth.

HER final summer was it.
XXVIII.

HOLLY AS UNFINISHED SUPERLATIVE

The cold reaches through the thinness of my one-bedroom apartment.

The heat still off thanks to a very frugal management, I sip lavender tea in one room while my partner reads in another, a comfortable quiet falling over our evening.

Autumn, a writer bundled at a desk, searching for clues. It's like this lately. Cold, quiet, hungry.

In my quest for Holly among the archives, I find a yearbook. 1959, the high school where Holly spent four years of her life.

Looking through the sepia glimpses of young Holly, I realize I have never seen a photo of her aside from the portrait my father anoints with oil.

In these photos, my grandmother is smiling.

She is in chorus, marching band, library club. Wearing a majorette costume.

She likes to read, write, act in school plays.

She coifs her blonde hair just so.

She wants to be a medical secretary. She wants to be a mother. She wants to grow old and be in love and see the world.

She has, without knowing it, already been through half of her life.

Holly

HOLLY AS AFTERNOON WALK IN OCTOBER

I amble beneath a throng of pigeons and power lines.

I turn on Braddock, purchase a warm loaf of bread and carry it in my arms with a sense of liability.

I think of calling my father and choose not to.

I think of what we choose and what we don't.

I think of children, the dream I had where my daughter woke me to ask for milk.

I think of waking as the death of that dream.

I think of waking as the absence of my grandmother.

I think of a broken ashtray.

I think of shattering.

I think of a boy

I think of a body

I think of a **boy** and a **body**

I think of a **boy** and a **body** and a **boy** and a **body** and a **boy** and a **body** &

NOTES

In *HOLLY AS MOURNING AND MELANCHOLY*, I include research and language from Sigmund Freud's 1917 essay "Mourning and Melancholia" as well as Judith Butler's 1995 paper "Melancholy Gender—Refused Identities" and Matthew Ratcliffe's 2017 article "Grief and the Unity of Emotion." The line "ontological incoherence is itself a form of grief" is a nod to Michael Sneideke's *Queer Optimism: Lyric Personhood and Other Felicitous Persuasions*.

I owe *HOLLY AS LEARNING METAPHOR* to Anne Carson, whose 1987 essay "Kinds of Water" was a source of inspiration for this piece. On that note, I owe much of my hybrid practice to Anne Carson.

In *HOLLY AS BOYS RUNNING IN TWO DIRECTIONS*, I reference Karen Green's 2013 hybrid text and image collection *Bough Down*, a book that fell off the shelf and made me an artist.

In *HOLLY AS FASHIONABLE NEIGHBORHOOD*, I pull etymological research from *Etymonline* and the *Oxford English Dictionary*.

HOLLY AS SURVEY OF QUESTIONS FOR THE SURVIVED is after CD Wright's poem "Breathtaken," in which she includes a section called "Petition to the Bearers of Precious Images to recollect a few things about him/her." This poem is in her 2016 collection, *Shallcross*, which she was finishing around the time when she passed away.

Collages include snippets from Dr. Carl Malmquist's 1986 study "Children Who Witness Parental Murder," articles from the *Watertown Daily Times*, and poems from Running Press Books's 1991 edition of *Emily Dickinson's Collected Poems*. Collages also include personal and family archival materials, Crayola fingerpaint, Case for Making watercolors, and other ephemera.

The structure of this book was inspired by Carmen Maria Machado's *In the Dream House* and by many others. I refused to read Maggie Nelson's *Jane* and *The Red Parts* until this book was finished, but when I did, I cried in recognition.

ACKNOWLEDGMENTS

Thank you to the *New Delta Review*, *Hayden's Ferry Review*, *Guesthouse*, *Fugue*, *petrichor journal*, and *Diode Editions* for publishing images and text from this book, sometimes in earlier versions.

Thank you to the many institutions that have supported the creation of this work. I'd specifically like to thank the residency program at Mass MoCA and to MCLA for hosting me as their inaugural Under 27 Writer-in-Residence Fellow in 2022. So much of this work was born in your studios. Thank you for giving me a chance.

Thank you to Dawn Lundy Martin, Jeanne Marie Laskas, and Diana Khoi Nguyen, who shepherded this book into being.

Thank you to YYB, and to KMA Sullivan and Gale Marie Thompson specifically, who held this book with such vision and care. And thank you to Katie Prince for her intuitive design work.

Thank you to Lytton Smith, who believed in me even when I didn't. Teaching is a thankless job that lives forever. Thank you for showing me that I am a poet.

I wrote this book because I love my family. This goes out to them.

I wrote this book because I am loved. Thank you to the many friends and artists in my life whom I call my community. Thank you to BW, forever and ever my steady place.

Thank you to CD and ED, poets no longer of this earth but of my heart.

Thank you, Susan, for always reading what I wrote. I love you and miss you, my queen of freaks.

Thank you to Ann Holliday, nicknamed "Holly," my grandmother, who has been gone for fifty years. You live in us.

GRACE (GE) GILBERT (they/them) is a poet, writer and collage artist. They are the author of *Holly* (YesYes Books, 2026) and three chapbooks. Work can be found in *Best of the Net Anthology 2023*, *Iowa Review*, *Pleiades*, *Foglifter*, *Indiana Review*, *Ninth Letter*, *Adroit Journal*, and elsewhere. They received their MFA in poetry from the University of Pittsburgh in 2022, where they now teach. They also teach hybrid collage and poetics courses at Brooklyn Poets, Minnesota Center for Book Arts, and other institutions. Learn more at gracegegilbert.com.

ALSO BY YESYES BOOKS

FICTION

The Nothing by Lauren Davis
Girls Like Me by Nina Packebush
Three Queerdos and a Baby by Nina Packebush
Book of Exemplary Women by Diana Xin

WRITING RESOURCES

Gathering Voices: Creating a Community-Based Poetry Workshop by Marty McConnell

FULL-LENGTH POETRY AND MIXED GENRE

Ugly Music by Diannely Antigua
Bone Language by Jamaica Baldwin
Cataloguing Pain by Allison Blevins
Strange Flowers by Bryan Byrdlong
What Runs Over by Kayleb Rae Candrilli
Don't Cut Your Own Bangs by Caroline Crew
This, Sisyphus by Brandon Courtney
sipèstisyon by Mckendy Fils-Aimé
Salt Body Shimmer by Aricka Foreman
Gutter by Lauren Brazeal Garza
Forever War by Kate Gaskin
Inconsolable Objects by Nancy Miller Gomez
Ceremony of Sand by Rodney Gomez
Loudest When Startled by luna rey hall
Everything Breaking / For Good by Matt Hart
Brine Orchid by Arah Ko
40 WEEKS by Julia Kolchinsky
murmurations by Anthony Thomas Lombardi
Sons of Achilles by Nabila Lovelace
Refusenik by Lynn Melnick
GOOD MORNING AMERICA I AM HUNGRY AND ON FIRE by jamie mortara
Born Backwards by Tanya Olson
a falling knife has no handle by Emily O'Neill
To Love an Island by Ana Portnoy Brimmer
Another Way to Split Water by Alycia Pirmohamed
Tell This to the Universe by Katie Prince
One God at a Time by Meghan Privitello
I'm So Fine: A List of Famous Men & What I Had On by Khadijah Queen
If the Future Is a Fetish by Sarah Sgro
Gilt by Raena Shirali
[insert] boy by Danez Smith
Say It Hurts by Lisa Summe

Hand Over Hand Over the Edge of the World
by Patrick Swaney
Boat Burned by Kelly Grace Thomas
Helen Or My Hunger by Gale Marie Thompson
As She Appears by Shelley Wong
Dead Boys in Space by Sara Youngblood Gregory

RECENT CHAPBOOK COLLECTIONS

Vinyl 45s

Exit Pastoral by Aidan Forster
Crown for the Girl Inside by Lisa Low
Phantasmagossip by Sara Mae
Year of the Sheep by Stacey Park
Scavenger by Jessica Lynn Suchon
Unmonstrous by John Allen Taylor
Giantess by Emily Vizzo

Blue Note Editions

Kissing Caskets by Mahogany L. Browne
One Above One Below: Positions & Lamentations
by Gala Mukomolova
The Porch (As Sanctuary) by Jae Nichelle
The Only Way Out Is Through by Katie Jean Shinkle

www.ingramcontent.com/pod-product-compliance
Lightning Source LLC
LaVergne TN
LVHW060635110826
845147LV00014B/913

* 9 7 8 1 9 4 6 3 0 3 1 7 2 *